THE G.I. SERIES

Custer and his Commands

Cadet Custer, West Point Class of 1861, was at the bottom of the academic list upon graduation with the most demerits and worst standing in terms of grades. He wears the gray coatee with brass ball buttons that was adopted in the early 1800s and in a similar form still serves as the United States Military Academy's dress uniform. *WPM*

THE G.I. SERIES

THE ILLUSTRATED HISTORY OF THE AMERICAN
SOLDIER, HIS UNIFORM AND HIS EQUIPMENT

Custer and his Commands

From West Point to Little Bighorn

Kurt Hamilton Cox

Pen & Sword
MILITARY

Custer and his Commands: From West Point to Little Bighorn

A Greenhill Book
First published in 1999 by Greenhill Books,
Lionel Leventhal Limited
www.greenhillbooks.com

This edition published in 2015 by
PEN & SWORD MILITARY
An imprint of
Pen & Sword Books Ltd
47 Church Street
Barnsley,
South Yorkshire
S70 2AS

Copyright © Lionel Leventhal Limited, 1999

ISBN: 978-1-84832-807-5

CIP data records for this title are available from the
British Library

Designed by DAG Publications Ltd
Design by David Gibbons
Layout by Anthony A. Evans

Printed and bound by in Malta by Gutenberg Press Ltd

Pen & Sword Books Ltd incorporates the Imprints
of Aviation, Atlas, Family History, Fiction, Maritime,
Military, Discovery, Politics, History, Archaeology,
Select, Wharncliffe Local History, Wharncliffe True
Crime, Military Classics, Wharncliffe Transport,
Leo Cooper, The Praetorian Press, Remember When,
Seaforth Publishing and Frontline Publishing.

For a complete list of Pen & Sword titles
please contact
PEN & SWORD BOOKS LIMITED
47 Church Street, Barnsley, South Yorkshire,
S70 2AS, England
E-mail: enquiries@pen-and-sword.co.uk
Website: www.pen-and-sword.co.uk

ACKNOWLEDGEMENTS AND ABBREVIATIONS

The author wishes to thank the individuals and staff
of the institutions noted below:

ABBREVIATIONS

BB	Dr Bill Benthem
CPSM	Colorado Springs Pioneer Museum, Colorado Springs, CO
EAL	Dr Elizabeth Atwood Lawrence
EGL	Edward G. Longacre
FAM	Frontier Army Museum, Fort Leavenworth, KS
GM	Greg Martin
GS	Glen Swanson
LBBNM	Little Big Horn Battlefield National Monument, Crow Agency, MT
LC	Library of Congress, Washington, DC
MJM	Dr Michael J. McAfee
NA	National Archives, College Park, MD
SHSND	State Historical Society of North Dakota, Bismarck, ND
SI	Smithsonian Institution, Museum of American History, Washington, DC
RMU	Robert M. Utley
USAMHI	US Army Military History Institute, Carlisle Barracks, PA
USAQM	US Army Quartermaster Museum, Ft Lee, Virginia
WC	Wes Clark
WP	US Military Academy Library, West Point, NY
YUL	Yale University Library, New Haven, CT

CUSTER AND HIS COMMANDS
FROM WEST POINT TO LITTLE BIGHORN

On 1 July 1857 the 17-year-old George Armstrong Custer reported to the United States Military Academy at West Point, New York. There the ruddy-faced youth donned the cadet gray – the first of many uniforms he would wear during his short, eventful martial career.

Enthusiastic, ambitious, and proud, Custer had the makings of a dashing soldier, although he lacked one quality of great importance to a warrior – discipline. Prone to practical jokes, and bent on enjoying himself during his West Point days, Cadet Custer seems to have spent more time in extracurricular activities than in applying himself to his studies. This resulted in poor grades and an incredible number of demerits. But Custer did excel in several military subjects, a point in his favor that soon would serve him well for, in April 1861, the sectional differences that had been smoldering for decades in the United States ignited into civil war.

Shortly after fighting erupted between the North and the South, Custer graduated as the 'goat' (the man with the lowest marks) of his class. On 24 June 1861 he received his commission as a second lieutenant of the Second U.S. Cavalry. The days of studying war in the classroom had come to an end. The real test for the young subaltern would be on the field of battle.

During his first few months in the field the new lieutenant hardly distinguished himself from the many others who fought for the Union. Gradually, though, he acquired combat experience, taking part in a number of skirmishes, and even went aloft in a hot air balloon to observe enemy operations.

These ventures assisted him in securing a promotion to first lieutenant on 17 July 1862, now serving with the Fifth U.S. Cavalry. Even before his formal promotion, Custer had gained a temporary upgrade to captain and an appointment as an aide-de-camp. This post brought him to the attention of the commander of the Army of the Potomac, Major General George B. McClellan, who described Custer as 'slim, long-haired... simply a reckless, gallant boy undeterred by fatigue, unconscious of fear... his head was always clear in danger and he always brought me clear and intelligible reports of what he saw under the heaviest fire.'

His superiors' recognition of his bravery and coolness in battle helped propel Custer rapidly upwards. On 29 June 1863, at the tender age of 23, he was promoted to brevet brigadier general of volunteers. Now Custer was living the life of the beplumed warrior horsemen of yore he had read about as a youth. Soon he began to look the part with flowing hair and flamboyant custom-made uniforms, though he also became a target of ridicule for this distinctive dress.

Custer's command was the Michigan Brigade (2nd Brigade, 3rd Division), a unit made up regiments from his adopted home state, and they were soon in the thick of battle with their new brigadier. Within weeks of joining his 'Wolverines', the 'Boy General', as the Northern press would dub him, blindly charged Confederate cavalry near Hunterstown, Pennsylvania, during the Gettysburg engagement. He lost 32 men, and his horse, which was shot out from under him, but gained an award for bravery.

Several months later Custer again faced J.E.B. Stuart's horsemen with distinction, this time capturing the dashing rebel cavalryman's headquarters. Custer was wounded in this engagement, however, and traveled to his family home in Monroe, Michigan, to recuperate. While he was convalescing he took the opportunity to conclude a successful courtship and win the hand of Elizabeth 'Libbie' Bacon, the daughter of a prominent local judge.

After a February 1864 wedding, Custer returned to duty. On 31 March he reported to a new superior, General Philip H. Sheridan, who was to exert great influence on his career thereafter. Within days he was back in the field. More victories came his way, although he had at least one narrow escape at the Battle of Trevilian Station where he was nearly captured by the Confederates.

But otherwise Custer's good fortune held, and his heroics gained him an appointment as major general of volunteers in command of the 3rd Division of the Army of the Potomac's Cavalry Corps. At this time Custer's younger brother Tom was transferred to George's staff, with a promotion from corporal to second lieutenant, and was given a post as an aide-de-camp. Nepotism or not, Tom earned considerable laurels in his own right, being twice decorated with the Medal of Honor – a rare distinction in U.S. combat annals then, or since. However, the family's conspicuous glory-gaining came to a halt after Robert E. Lee's surrender in early April 1865.

With the war over the Custers were stationed briefly in Richmond, Virginia, where they lodged for a short time in Jefferson Davis' former residence. Then George was transferred to a new command at Hempstead, Texas. Custer's father, Emanuel, and brother Tom joined 'Autie' (Custer's childhood nickname) and Libbie there. Once more Tom was posted as his brother's aide, while their father took an appointment as a civilian forage master. Despite being surrounded by his family in this way, the assignment turned sour for Custer who proved a less able peacetime leader than wartime commander. He was seemingly poorly equipped to deal with the problems of disciplining troops who were citizen soldiers anxious to return home and many of his men in Texas held him in low esteem.

Adding to Custer's woes was the fact that, with the end of the Civil War, the army faced a large-scale reduction in its strength. Many officers and men were forced to leave the service, while others, including Custer, had to accept considerable downgrades in rank.

Custer was told he he would revert to a captaincy in the Fifth Cavalry and quickly set off to Washington to pull strings and arrange a better billet. He met with Secretary of War Edwin Stanton to petition for Regular Army commissions for himself, his brother Tom, and his comrade George Yates. In addition Custer also explored civilian alternatives to U.S. military service and even toyed with an offer of $16,000 a year (then a princely sum and double his major general's pay) to become adjutant general of the Mexican Army!

Still unsure of what to do, Custer joined President Andrew Johnson's tour of the country to rally the nation around his Reconstruction policies. In the process Custer began to think about politics, especially a Congressional career, as another road to fulfil his aspirations. Then, on 28 July 1866, destiny dictated otherwise. On that date he accepted the lieutenant colonelcy of the Seventh U.S. Cavalry.

In October Autie and Libbie Custer left the grand circle of the president and his entourage for their new home at Fort Riley, Kansas, where recruits for the regiment were gathering. Officially Colonel Andrew J. Smith was the unit's commanding officer, but in reality Custer would remain in effective control of the regiment for the next decade.

Custer's tenure in command began with a spell of drill and other mundane garrison duties, but this routine ended in March 1867. Custer was to take to the field on his first campaign against Native Americans. General Winfield S. Hancock was gathering forces, including the Seventh, for an expedition against Cheyennes and other groups of native people.

Observers soon noted Custer's self-confidence in his new role, though in fact the regiment achieved little success in what turned out to be a long and fruitless chase after the Cheyenne. Custer became very critical of Hancock's methods and was also unhappy about being parted for so long from his wife. Ultimately he was brought before a court martial for leaving his command without permission and sentenced to a year's suspension from pay and service.

Yet the winds of war wrested Custer out of his exile before he had served his punishment. Once more Sheridan had plans to send the Seventh into the field against the Southern Cheyenne. On 27 November 1868 this foray brought Custer and some 800 troopers to the frozen banks of the Washita River in today's Oklahoma. In the freezing early morning the men removed their heavy kersey overcoats in preparation to attack a large village while its occupants still slept. The regimental band struck up the famous cavalry march tune *Garry Owen* while the cavalrymen fell on the village with a vengeance, until fears that a arge body of enemy reinforcements would arrive o join the fray brought a withdrawal.

When the fighting concluded the troopers had laimed 103 warriors killed (plus an unknown number of women and children), as well as taking some 53 non-combatants captive. Additionally, Custer ordered a sizeable pony herd of 875 mounts destroyed. Without these horses and the over 1,000 buffalo skins, hundreds of pounds of black powder, and all the weapons seized in the fight, the Cheyennes' ability to make war was reduced considerably.

This victory was not without its cost. Two officers and 19 men were killed and three officers and 11 men were wounded. These casualties were mainly from a detachment under Major Joel Elliot whom Custer had sent in separately when he split the regiment to strike the village. Exactly who was to blame for the death of Elliot and his detachment was a question that caused a rift in the command which remained ever after. Some thought that Custer had abandoned Elliot and his men to their fate. Moreover, Custer's failure to learn the consequences of dividing his unit without adequate communication between the various columns likewise would come back to haunt the Seventh. For the time being, though, Custer was praised by his superiors, while he and the Seventh came to be seen as premier Indian fighters, a task that they fulfilled until March 1871.

The order announcing the regiment's reassignment noted, 'During the four years which it has been in this Department [of the Missouri] it has experienced all of the hardships, dangers and vicissitudes attendant upon military operations on our wild frontier. It has made many long and toilsome marches exposed to the severest storms of winter, and has gone for days in that inclement season without shelter and almost without food for man or animal.'

After experiencing such deprivations, many men in the regiment no doubt rejoiced to learn that their new posting would be to the Department of the South. Scattered among seven Southern states as a sort of adjunct to the Department of Justice, the troopers provided a back-up for the U.S. Marshals who labored to see that Reconstruction policies were carried out in the face of such formidable opposition as the night-riding Ku Klux Klan that had been formed after the Civil War.

After two years of this constabulary duty, the Seventh was again slated for redeployment, this time to Texas. Growing tensions on the Northern Great Plains dictated otherwise and instead the regiment regrouped and concentrated at Yankton, Dakota Territory, with the exception of its colonel, Samuel D. Sturgis, who went to St. Paul, Minnesota, on detached service, and two companies under Major Marcus Reno which were detailed to escort an international commission setting the boundary line between Canada and the United States.

While Reno's squadron undertook this responsibility, Custer and the remainder of the companies set out from their new posts in the Dakotas on an expedition to the Yellowstone country. Custer and a detachment of 90 men fought two minor engagements in the course of August 1873, one near what ultimately became the site of Fort Keogh, Montana, and the other by the Yellowstone River near its junction with the Little Bighorn. Afterwards, the Seventh experienced no further opposition for the remainder of the year.

This period of calm continued until the summer of 1874, when Custer again set out, this time from Fort Abraham Lincoln, Dakota Territory, and headed for the Black Hills. This area was considered sacred by the Sioux people and supposedly protected by treaty from white incursion. Thus Custer's expedition was seen as a hostile act. Custer's expedition was supposedly being mounted to escort a civilian scientific mission to study the zoology, geology, and paleontology of the region. In fact scientific inquiries took a distant second place to their efforts to ascertain whether precious minerals were to be found in the Black Hills area. The answer was a resounding yes.

When the news that gold was found in the Black Hills was made public, a mass immigration of prospectors immediately began, despite the fact that their presence there was illegal and they officially faced ejection if caught in the area by the army. In the summer of 1875 Custer's men were deployed to keep the miners and prospectors out of the treaty lands. The army's efforts to police the treaty were half-hearted at best and many gold seekers avoided detection by the cavalrymen, though some were intercepted and killed by the Sioux and Cheyennes. The Indians refused to give up their hunting grounds, while the whites would not respect treaty guarantees with the lure of riches being so strong. Officials in Washington determined to take action in favor of the mining interests.

Custer in the meantime had alienated the administration of U.S. Grant, who had been elected president after the Civil War, and his request to lead the Seventh into the field was denied. Again Custer called upon powerful allies to be allowed to join the regiment. Sheridan and others secured Custer's reinstatement, but in so doing inadvertently signed his death warrant.

Unaware of what was ahead, Custer reported back to Fort Lincoln where he joined Brigadier General Alfred Terry's command. Their mission was to locate the thousands of Sioux, Cheyenne, and Arapaho, led by the likes of Sitting Bull and Crazy Horse, who had ignored the government's order that they were to be confined to reservations. The column rode out to immortality on 17 May 1876.

The enemy remained elusive until 15 June when Major Reno, returning from a scout, reported he had found signs of a large hostile movement near the Rosebud River. Terry instructed Custer to take the Seventh and follow this trail until the enemy camp was located. While Custer pressed forward, Terry's main command was to continue on, with the intention of reuniting on 26 June for a strike against the hostiles.

On 22 June the Seventh set out find the enemy. By a series of rapid day and night marches the command reached the divide between the Rosebud and Little Bighorn Rivers. Scouts reported the presence of the encampment, but additional intelligence indicated that the inhabitants knew the army was at their door. Custer had 'Officer's Call' sounded and gave orders for a three-pronged attack. He divided the regiment into three squadrons, one with five troops under his own control, and two with three troops each under Reno and Benteen.

The events that followed became one of the most debated and controversial military engagements in U.S. history. In the end, one fact is clear. Custer and over 225 of his men went down in defeat to overwhelming numbers of Sioux and Cheyenne warriors. Benteen's and Reno's commands would survive by digging in on high ground, ignorant of the fate of their commanding officer, until Terry arrived with reinforcements on 27 June to find the stripped, mutilated bodies of the dead scattered under the broiling Montana sun.

The death of Custer and his men was pronounced a massacre. After hastily burying the dead and transporting the wounded back to Fort Lincoln, the decimated regiment was scarcely allowed to rest. The news of 'Custer's Last Stand' flashed eastward, and the regiment was reconstituted. Its authorized strength was raised to 1,200 officers and men, nearly double that when the unit rode into the valley of death.

Over the next decade Custer's old command remained active, and faced Native Americans a number of times until December 1890 when, at a cold, lonely place called Wounded Knee, a squadron of the Seventh surrounded a haggard group of Sioux. On 29 December 1890, while the troops were demanding the surrender of arms from the 100 or so men in the village, a weapon was leveled and fired. No one really knows who fired this first shot but the army's reaction was crushing. The Sioux were massacred by fire from the cavalrymen and the Hotchkiss guns of the Second U.S. Artillery. Mass graves were dug for 146 men, women, and children, with an unknown number of other casualties having been taken away by family and friends, or having moved off on their own to die later. Captain George Wallace, a veteran of 1876, and 21 other soldiers also died, many of them probably shot by their own side by mistake. The tragic Wounded Knee affair, like Little Bighorn, would take on many meanings but it was at last the concluding chapter in the history of the Seventh U.S. Cavalry's clashes with Native Americans.

FOR FURTHER READING

Barnett, Louise, *Touched By Fire: The Life, Death, and Mythic Afterlife of George Armstrong Custer*. New York: Henry Holt and Company, 1996.

Chandler, Melbourne C., *Of Garryowen In Glory: The History of the 7th U.S. Cavalry*. N.P. Melbourne C. Chandler, 1960.

Graham, W.A., *The Custer Myth: A Source Book of Custeriana*. Mechanicsburg, PA: Stackpole Books, 1995.

Katz, D. Mark., *Custer in Photographs*. New York: Bonanza Books, 1985.

Urwin, Gregory J.W., *Custer Victorious: The Civil War Battles of George Armstrong Custer*. Lincoln: University of Nebraska Press, 1990.

Soon after he was promoted to a Union generalship, Custer's red scarf became one of his trademarks. A wide sailor-type collar with stars also often formed part of his distinctive garb as a dashing commander of Yankee cavalry. *GS*

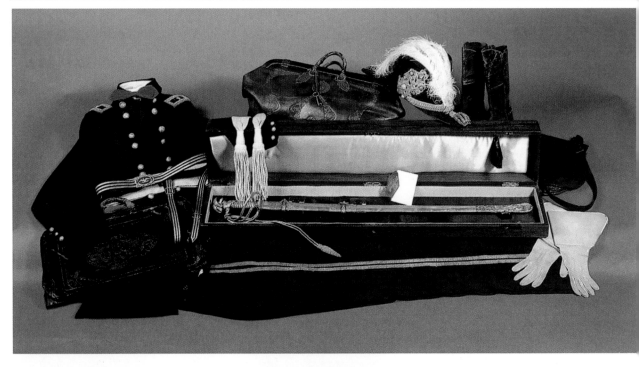

Above: During 11 and 12 June 1864, at the Battle of Trevilian Station, Custer's personal baggage wagon fell into enemy hands. Among captured treasures was his brigadier general's dress uniform (which he probably wore at his wedding the previous February) including his *chapeau de bras*, custom gold lace belt, gauntlets, and elegant Tiffany presentation sword. Many of these items appear in various portrait photos that Custer had taken by Brady and others prior to their capture. *Photo by Gary Donihoo. WC*

Left: Detail of Custer's presentation saber captured at the Battle of Trevilian Station. *Photo by Gary Donihoo. WC*

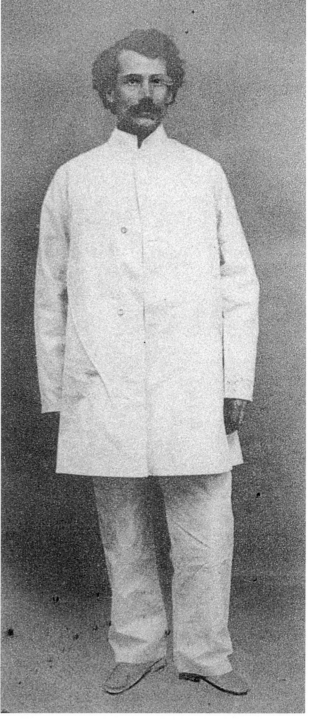

Above: The formal uniform worn by Custer's Seventh Cavalry troopers from 1866 to 1872 included a hat brim pinned on the left, although by regulations the brims of cavalry hats were to be looped up on the right. *USAQM*

Above right: This pattern of the long single-breasted white canvas stable-frock closed with three buttons. It had been adopted as early as the 1850s. These garments were issued to mounted troops (cavalry and light artillery) to keep their more expensive wool uniforms from being soiled. The canvas could be washed easily, a necessary requirement because the color undoubtedly showed the dirt inevitably associated with grooming horses, cleaning stalls, and the other chores associated with maintaining a mount. *USAQM*

Above: In 1873 the dismounted overcoat with a matching second cape attached for additional warmth was prescribed for all troops. It is possible that enlisted men of the Seventh Cavalry were issued this garment, but it is not known if they were. These were Civil War surplus garments that were converted to a new style but were only used for a scant few years until a new design greatcoat was produced in 1876, though it is also uncertain whether these were issued to the Seventh Cavalry. *USAQM*

Above: The well-dressed Seventh Cavalry enlisted man was to don a new dress uniform after major changes in patterns were prescribed in 1872. Old accoutrements of Civil War vintage, however, continued to be used in tandem with the new dress uniform for several years thereafter. *USAQM*

An 1872-pattern cavalry private's coat and helmet with horsetail plume. Brass numerals were affixed to each side of the collar to designate the wearer's regiment. All enlisted men were issued these uniform items for dress wear. *GS*

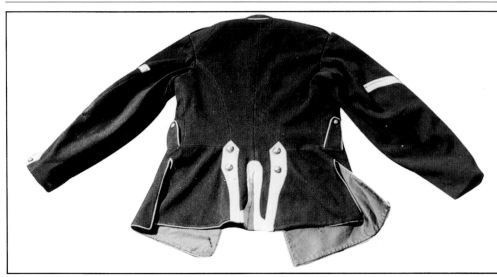

Left: The rear of an 1872-pattern enlisted dress coat, in this case belonging to Sergeant William Williams, Seventh U.S. Cavalry. The skirts of the first production models of these coats were lined in yellow, but this practice was discontinued soon after the coats were adopted. *LBBNM*

Below: Captain Frederick Benteen more than likely wore this 1872-pattern folding hat on the 1876 expedition to the Little Bighorn, as he had in previous campaigns. The pocket knife, watch fob, and other items were also his. *GS*

Opposite page, top: Major Marcus Reno's forage cap formed part of his garrison uniform. The bag and tintype also belonged to Reno. *GS*

Opposite page, bottom: A pair of sabers, a Native American carrying case, and a captain's 1872-pattern dress knot which belonged to Captain Thomas McDougall. McDougall commanded the regimental pack train during the Little Bighorn campaign and joined up with Reno and Benteen after Custer and his command had been wiped out. *GS*

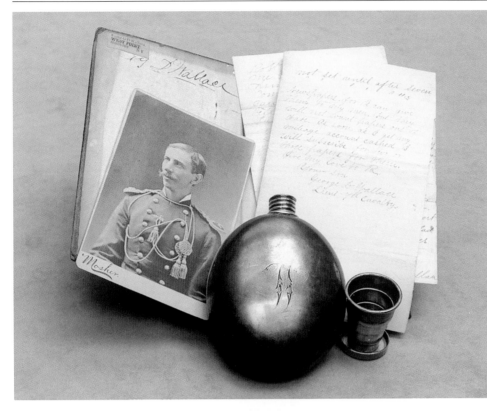

Left: Second Lieutenant Daniel Wallace attached the end of his 1872-pattern helmet cords to a pin displaying the regimental numeral above crossed sabers as seen in this cabinet photograph. Wallace's flask and the manuscript account of one of his Western field experiences are also shown. *GS*

Below: Custer's 1872-pattern plumed helmet was his crowning glory, but is seldom seen in any of the photographs he had taken of himself. *SI, Museum of American History*

Here Custer wears the cadet forage cap that presaged a similar style of enlisted man's forage cap which began to be issued in the late 1850s. Black stripes ornament the winter gray trousers while black mohair piping adorns the matching cadet gray coatee. *National Portrait Gallery, SI*

Above: On 20 May 1862 the youthful Second Lieutenant Custer of the Fifth U.S. Cavalry was serving as a member of General Andrew Porter's staff, Custer (lying down beside the dog) wears the uniform of a company grade officer with a single-breasted nine button frock coat as its main component, topped by the plain shoulder straps with yellow centers which designated second lieutenants of cavalry. *LC*

Below: In this June 1863 image taken with General Alfred Pleasonton at Falmouth, Virginia, Captain Custer (left) has exchanged his frock coat for a 'stable jacket', a short garment allowed for use by mounted officers. A typical cavalry trooper of the Civil War appears at attention in the background wearing a four-button sack coat and forage cap with stamped sheet brass insignia on the crown, a rather typical although non-regulation arrangement. *LC*

For this 8 October 1863 portrait Custer, as a recently promoted brigadier general of volunteers, wears the double-breasted rock coat with eight buttons in each row grouped in twos, as called for by regulations for officers of his rank. The collar and the cuffs were to be midnight blue velvet. The buttons are not the staff officer's pattern that were usually worn by general officers, but instead appear to be standard line officer's versions. The shoulder straps have gold embroidered outer borders and a silver star on a black or dark blue background. *NA*

Above: Gold galloons, additions of his own selection, ornament Brigadier General Custer's sleeves (far right) in this 9 October 1863 photo taken with General Pleasonton (seated beside Custer) and other Union officers, both regulars and volunteers, at Warrenton, Virginia. The officer standing in the center, First Lieutenant George Whitehead of the Sixth Pennsylvania Cavalry, has his sash 'scarf style' across the chest. This was correct for the officer of the day.

Most of the officers have elected to obtain short stable jackets, although the one on the far left, Sixth U.S. Cavalry First Lieutenant Benjamin Hutchins, has on a four-button sack coat. The first lieutenant standing behind General Pleasonton is George Yates of the Fourth Michigan Cavalry. After the Civil War he secured a regular army commission with Custer and the Seventh Cavalry. *LC*

Left: Captain Manning D. Birge of the Sixth Michigan Volunteer Cavalry has turned up the side of his slouch hat and added a pair of bars to the crown to indicate his rank, although he also wears the appropriate shoulder straps for this same purpose. *EGL*

Below: George G. Briggs, who ultimately commanded the Seventh Michigan Volunteer Cavalry under Custer, started his Civil War as a junior officer as seen here when he was a first lieutenant in the regiment. Note the regimental number above the crossed sabres cavalry officer's hat insignia. The hat itself has a lower crown than the regulation 1858 pattern. *EGL*

Opposite page, bottom: Brigadier General Custer's staff of the Michigan Cavalry Brigade depict typical examples of the varied uniforms donned by Union officers during the Civil War. Custer (seated, in front of the door) has added a single star to his civilian slouch hat and has a single gold stripe on the outer seams of his trousers, as opposed to the double gold stripes he wore on some of his other trousers after being elevated to brigadier general. The soldier in the left foreground wears the 1851-pattern mounted sky blue kersey enlisted man's overcoat. On the porch, Sergeant Michael Butler holds Custer's personal flag with white crossed sabers on a red upper and blue lower field. Butler wears the blue wool cavalry enlisted jacket with yellow worsted tape trim adopted in 1855. *LBBNM*

Right: Colonel Thornton F. Broadhead, commanding officer of the First Michigan Cavalry, wears the 1851-pattern officer's cloakcoat over his 1851-pattern field grade officer's double-breasted frock coat. *EGL*

Opposite page: As a major general Custer not only wore shoulder straps bearing two silver five-pointed stars, but also obtained a new double-breasted frock coat with nine buttons in each row grouped in threes, as called for by regulations for officers of that rank. Custer was named a brevet major general of volunteers in October 1864. *GS*

Left: William D. Mann, lieutenant colonel of the Fifth Michigan Volunteer Cavalry and later colonel of the Seventh Michigan, poses here in an 1851-pattern officer's overcoat worn over his 1851-pattern field grade officer's frock coat. *EGL*

Right: Custer's rank of major general was indicated both by regulation shoulder straps and his own addition of two silver stars (one of which can be seen here) applied to the crown of his broad-brimmed campaign hat. Note the cravat that was an optional accessory allowed by regulations. Usually these neckties were black, but Custer is also known to have had scarlet ones. *LC*

Below: Major General George Custer is joined by his wife, Elizabeth Bacon Custer, and his aide, brother Thomas Ward Custer, who appears with the shoulder straps of a second lieutenant attached to a tailored four-button sack with slash pocket at the breast. Note the gold general officer's hat cords that terminate in acorn devices on George Custer's hat. *NA*

Opposite page: A light blue shirt with broad collar having stars and piping applied, flowing red scarf, gauntlets, high polished boots, and a custom double-breasted frock with exterior pockets set off Major General Custer's wavy locks as he adopted the look of a dashing cavalier for this 23 May 1865 Matthew Brady portrait. *LC*

Left: The Third Division, (Sheridan's) Cavalry Corps, Army of the Potomac, adopted their division commander's red kerchief and a five pointed star above a Maltese cross in gold and blue as their corps badge. Here the badge is seen worn by Custer. *Museum of American History, SI*

Below: George Custer ('Autie') is joined by Mrs Carrie Farnham Lyon at Hempstead, Texas, on 18 October 1865. With the Civil War over, Custer now served on Reconstruction duty in the South. He has given up his former black slouch for a lighter broad-brimmed 'planter's hat' that was more suitable to the local climate. The lighter blue collar of his shirt, no doubt hand-made by his loving wife, continues to be worn over the collar of the dark blue specially-made major general's coat that was a shorter version than the regulation style, this example somewhat resembling a Navy 'peacoat'. *LBBNM*

Above: Custer put aside his slouch hat for a forage cap as seen in this November 1865 gathering at his Austin, Texas, headquarters. Wife Libbie and brother Tom are seated on either side of George, and father Emanuel (seated back right) is among the others in the party. The officer seated on the step at the right front is Lieutenant Colonel Jacob Greene, who has a modified field officer's double-breasted frock coat with seven buttons in each row, according to regulations, but has added an outside pocket midway between the chest and waist. He also seems to have a gold cord instead of the regulation leather chin strap on his forage cap. Note that Tom Custer has double gold stripes on his trousers, once again a departure from regulations and, as was often the case, mimicking his older sibling. *LBBNM*

Right: Major General and Mrs Custer appear in a more formal portrait, this time from September 1866, where both wear versions of the blue and gold badge adopted by Autie's cavalry corps during the late Civil War. They were at this time making the grand tour with President Andrew Johnson while he made his bid for election. *LBBNM*

Left: Lieutenants Edward Settle Godfrey, Francis Marion Gibson, and Edward Law (left to right) have on the typical garb of junior officers for the period when the Seventh U.S. Cavalry was forming in Kansas, during 1866. Godfrey and Gibson pose in the regulation 1851–72 company officer's dark blue single-breasted frock coat with nine gilt buttons, while Law has obtained a heavy double-breasted civilian jacket that seems suitable for campaign service. Law and Godfrey both have the officer's type *chasseur* forage cap with embroidered gold crossed sabers for cavalry and silver regimental numeral. *LBBNM*

Right: First Lieutenants James Montgomery Bell (left) and William Winer Cooke (right) pose on either side of Captain Myles Moylan in a view taken at Fort Leavenworth, Kansas *circa* 1870. All wear the *chasseur* style forage cap that would become regulation in 1872, as well as the 1861-pattern sky-blue wool trousers piped with a ⅛-inch yellow welt. The only other concession to military uniforming is Bell's fatigue coat. Civilian clothing otherwise predominates. *GS*

Right: In another image dating from the Seventh Cavalry's early years, Captain Owen Hale of Company K wears the company grade officer's nine-button frock coat with its stand collar turned to reveal the black collar lining and his large cravat. It is interesting to note that the *chasseur*-style forage cap is identical to the type that would be adopted as regulation in 1872, right down to the front cap insignia. The thin gold cord was typical but not regulation until 1883, leather ones being the prescribed strap before that time. Such deviations from regulations were not uncommon in the Seventh Cavalry or any other regiment serving in the American West after the Civil War. 'Holy Owen' was on detached service in 1876, but was killed the next year fighting the Nez Percé. *GS*

Left: A bemused Tom Custer peers down upon James Calhoun to his right and Thomas Mower McDougall, to his left. McDougall still has his infantry forage cap, having not yet replaced it with a new one after his transfer from the Fifth U.S. Volunteer Infantry to join the Seventh Cavalry. Custer has added specially made insignia with oak leaves, evidently to denote his wartime brevet as a major. McDougall wears the nine button company grade officer's frock coat. His light blue trousers are piped with the infantry officer's ⅛-inch dark blue welt. The trouser cuffs (bottoms) are kept in place by stirrups. Calhoun is in civilian garb, except for his officer's trousers. *GS*

Right: First Lieutenant Algernon 'Fresh' Smith displays an extravagant white cravat on his 1872 dress uniform, as was permitted for officers by regulation. Such deviations from the standard uniform were common among officers at the time, as any opportunity to demonstrate a degree of individuality was exploited to the full. *GS*

Left: In one more variation on the same theme Captain George Yates of Company F, or the 'Band Box Troop' as it was sometimes called, has obtained a civilian jacket with black frogs and fleece-lined lapels and collar, plus pockets as a functional winter field garment in lieu of the regulation frock coat or four-button sack. He has also selected gauntlets and high boots for field use, while the jaunty but less practical *chasseur* forage cap tops off this outfit of the late 1860s through early 1870s. The ⅛-inch yellow welt for officers can be seen on his trousers. *LBBNM*

Right: In another 'fashion statement' Yates has donned a 'pillbox' cap with crossed saber insignia and gold cap cord. Although such caps were non-regulation, their association with British officers serving in the far-flung parts of the empire appealed to some in the American military. Again a civilian jacket is pressed into service as a martial garment. *GS*

Left: Unlike in the other pictures, in this instance Yates wears the complete regulation full dress of cavalry company grade officers of the 1861–72 period, including epaulets. The coat is single-breasted with nine gilt buttons down the front, the sash is crimson, and the trousers sky-blue with an ⅛-inch welt let into the outer seams in yellow. Yates' cravat was an optional accessory. The 1858-pattern hat with two ostrich feathers for company grade officers and three for field grade officers was prescribed by regulations for dress occasions. It was to be looped on the right side and the brim on that side held in place by an embroidered 'Arms of the United States' device, while the front of the hat was to bear a gold embroidered crossed saber insignia surmounted by a silver '7' to indicate the regiment. Gold and black hat cords terminating in acorns completed this headpiece. *LBBNM*

Above: Captain Myles Walter Keogh of Company I wears a variation of the officer's 1858-pattern hat, similar to a style known as the 'Burnside hat', in reference to the Civil War Union general of the same name. The remainder of Keogh's pre-1872 outfit is regulation, although he wears his papal decorations in full size and miniature, as well as a XV Corps badge from the Civil War. *EL*

Above: Captain Albert Barnitz has set aside most regulation wear for his field outfit in this 1868 image. Only the trousers, crimson silk sash, saber, and saber belt are regulation, but the piped shirt, high boots, gauntlets, and plain slouch hat without insignia are typical purchased non-regulation items that were better suited for campaigns. *RMU*

Above: The Seventh Cavalry's early deployment was to various Kansas garrisons, including Fort Wallace where, on 26 June 1867, officers sat for a photo in front of the adjutant's office. Lieutenant James Bell (seated to the right) was the fort's commander. Bell's light cavalry saber is at his side. Also seen is Captain Albert Barnitz, seated in the center in a civilian style slouch hat favored by troops serving in the West. The remainder of the officers have the low crowned *chasseur* pattern forage caps that had gained popularity during the Civil War. To Barnitz's right an infantry lieutenant holds a Spencer carbine while the officer standing next to the door, probably First Lieutenant F.H. Beecher, Third U.S. Infantry, grasps a Henry lever-action rifle. Three enlisted men in the 1855-pattern cavalry jacket are also seen in the background, two with forage caps and a third with what is possibly the 1858-pattern enlisted man's hat with all the brass insignia removed. *YUL*

Right: His court martial over, Custer has been joined by family and friends for this group portrait taken at Fort Leavenworth, Kansas, in late 1867 or early 1868. Custer still wears his major general's wartime rank on the shoulders, indicated by two silver embroidered stars in the same fashion as they were placed on shoulder straps. His permanent rank as the lieutenant colonel of the Seventh Cavalry can be seen on the upper portions of the lapels of his civilian style 'Albert' coat, to which he has added insignia and what are probably gilt staff or general officer's buttons arranged as was regulation for a major general, two rows of nine buttons in groups of three. *LBBNM*

Left: Major Joel Elliot wears a field grade officer's frock coat with the collar turned back to expose the dark velvet lining. He has on the light colored vest (waistcoat) permitted by regulations for officers, and a necktie. Elliot would be killed at the Washita. The circumstances of his death contributed to a rift in the regiment. *GS*

Below: September 1869 found Custer, his friends, and fellow officers encamped near Big Dry Creek, Kansas, ostensibly to hunt buffalo. While the others are clothed in casual civilian styles, Custer relaxes in trademark buckskins with his newspaper. *LBBNM*

Opposite page: An impromptu officers' mess during the 1874 Black Hills Expedition reveals an officer in the foreground wearing the 1872-pattern campaign hat with broad brim hooked up and with his dark trousers carefully reinforced in the seat with a light-colored material, probably canvas. Also of note is his use of brogans instead of the more typical boots. Despite being far beyond the pale of civilization, the enlisted man in the background has on a white jacket befitting a waiter in an Eastern city's restaurant. *LBBNM*

This extraordinary image was taken on 13 August 1874 during the Black Hills expedition and shows Custer, other officers, including Captain Frederick Benteen (seated third right), and civilians of the mission. Clearly evident is the vast range of garb, both civilian and military, that was used in the field. Apparently, only Custer (lying down, center) and Captain William Ludlow (first on left) wear buckskin. Both Captain Ludlow and Lieutenant Custer (third from left) wear leggings. The officer to Tom Custer's left has donned a bib-front shirt popular with firemen, frontiersmen, and other non-military men of the period as well as some officers. Of the 29 military men in the photo, eleven wear the 1872-pattern campaign hat, eight wear the 1872-pattern forage cap, and the remaining ten wear civilian slouch hats. Most wear some sort of neckerchief or scarf, while almost all wear the regulation trousers. *GS*

Above: In the vicinity of the Little Heart River, a short ride from Fort Abraham Lincoln, Custer (center) and his favored officers relax during this July 1875 outing. Gone is the Civil War era look of the Washita Campaign, the officers now being seasoned campaigners and quite at ease in 'plainsman' attire. Custer's coat is the one rarely seen in photos of the era, while his nephew Boston (fourth from left) apparently wears his much used campaign buckskin. Note that Tom Custer (second from right) apes his brother's choice in headgear. *NA*

Below: Custer is bareheaded in this November 1873 group portrait taken on the steps of his quarters at Fort Abraham Lincoln, Dakota Territory, while both Captain William Thompson (leaning against the banister) and First Lieutenant James Calhoun (behind Custer) have on forage caps rather than helmets. In Calhoun's case the cap has a water-resistant removable cover. *SHSND*

In 1872 the 1858-pattern hat gave way to a new helmet for cavalry officers which bore the Arms of the United States in gilt metal with a silver regimental numeral superimposed on the shield. Custer has placed his helmet on a table next to him, and assumes the guise of a knight errant with his flowing plume, moustache, and long hair in this 1873 image. The outfit is the 1872-pattern field grade dress uniform of a lieutenant colonel of the Seventh Cavalry. The gold lace ornamentation on his cuffs is far larger than that called for by regulations of the time, the prescribed width being ¼-inch, but in Custer's case the lace is approximately ½-inch. Custer's manner of draping his gold chest cords is also non-regulation. *GS*

Above: This image showing the porch of Custer's quarters was taken in July 1875. Custer (seated far right) has once more removed his helmet, chest cords, and saber belt, and simply wears the forage cap with his dress uniform. Custer and many of his officers seemingly favored this combination for off-duty hours, as seen here. However, Tom Custer (far left first row) wears an 1872-pattern officer's fatigue blouse instead of the dress coat, as does Captain Stephen Baker of the Sixth U.S. Infantry (seated front row, right). Baker also wears the infantry hunting horn insignia that remained regulation until 1875 when it was replaced by crossed rifles. *LBBNM*

Left: During March 1876, while on leave in New York Custer sat for José M. Mora. The coat is not the one Custer wears in other pictures, in that the width of the gold lace on the sleeves is ¼-inch per regulations rather than the wider lace he had sewn to his coat in earlier images. Did he purchase this coat in New York during this trip, or did he borrow the whole outfit for the photo session? The latter possibility seems plausible, especially in light of closer examination of the helmet by Custer's side. It bears a silver '8' not the '7' that was correctly affixed to Custer's helmet in a previous 1873 portrait, and is on his helmet which survives in the collection of the Smithsonian Institution's Museum of American History. *GS*

Right: Taken in April 1876, just a few months before his death, Custer again drapes his gold chest cord in a distinctive, non-regulation fashion. His field grade officer's gold lace belt with eagle belt plate can be seen, as can a portion of his Military Order of the Loyal Legion of the U.S. medal, a decoration presented by a veterans' organization in an era prior to campaign medals being issued by the federal government. *GS*

Left: First Lieutenant James Montgomery Bell, Company D, wears his dress uniform with the 1872-pattern officer's forage cap, a combination that was permitted for off-duty occasions. Officers frequently purchased caps with the insignia embroidered in silver wire bullion directly to the cap, as seen here. The rather thin gold bullion chinstrap was typical of a type that would not become regulation until 1883, although it was favored by many before that date. Note the white 'berlin' gloves and stiff detachable collar and cuffs. Bell was on leave of absence at the time of the Little Bighorn battle. *GS*

Opposite page, top left: Canadian-born First Lieutenant William Winer Cooke was adjutant of the Seventh. Here he has removed all indications of rank from his 1872-pattern officer's dress coat, having buttoned it open to reveal its velvet-lined collar and his white bow tie. The metal clips on his shoulder are to hold his 1872-pattern shoulder knots. Cooke was killed at Little Bighorn. *LBBNM*

Opposite page, top right: As adjutant Cooke wore a more complex set of shoulder knots than other officers in the regiment, the right one having an aiguillette attached to it. *LBBNM*

Above: Captain Frederick Benteen was pugnacious and stood squarely in the opposite camp from his commanding officer. He has altered a standard 1851-pattern mounted enlisted man's overcoat by adding a warm fur collar to this sky-blue kersey garment to provide an inexpensive field expedient. *GS*

Right: First Lieutenant James Calhoun of Company C wears a white cravat with a wing collar. Calhoun's shoulder knots have large rather inelegant 'paddles'. Calhoun was Custer's brother-in-law and was killed in action on 25 June 1876. *GS*

Left: Cooke's right 1872-pattern epaulet had the aiguillettes attached permanently. *Photograph by Gordon Chappell. CSPM*

Below: Detail of the end of Cooke's aiguillettes. *CSPM*

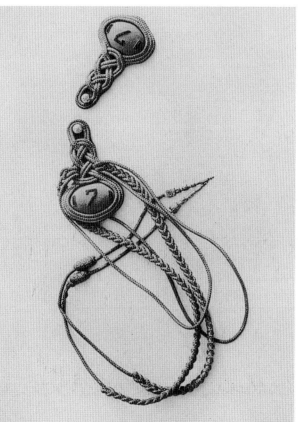

Left: Tom Custer, while still a first lieutenant, wears his two Medals of Honor, symbols of his valorous deeds during the Civil War, on his 1872-pattern company grade officer's uniform. Note the variation in the method of wearing his helmet cords. He would die alongside his brother. *LBBNM*

Left: Tom Custer wore his 1872-pattern folding hat *chapeau de bras* style in this photograph. He has the 1872-pattern officer's blouse with its black mohair frogging, but without the prescribed shoulder straps to designate his rank. The gauntlets bear a cryptic message 'K.O. 22d' the meaning of which remains a mystery. He holds an M1859 Light Cavalry Officer's Saber. *USAMHI*

Right: Company B's First Lieutenant William Thomas Craycroft sports a rather large black tie outside his stand collar. His saber is not regulation, and appears to be of European origin. The skirts of his 1872-pattern company grade officer's coat are also fairly short, as was not uncommon for mounted officers of the period. Craycroft was on detached service in June 1876. *GS*

Left: First Lieutenant Charles Camilius DeRudio of Company E was born in Italy. Sometimes called 'The Count' because of his personality and family background, DeRudio wears the officer's version of the 1872-pattern dress helmet. Minor differences distinguished the headgear worn by officers from those issued to the men, although variations from manufacturer to manufacturer existed as well. Shown here is the more complicated chinstrap of the officer's model. Also evident is the saber belt for company grade officers which was faced with gold lace interwoven with three silk stripes in the branch of service color, here yellow for cavalry, although appearing black due to the photographic process of the time. *GS*

Right: Here DeRudio has replaced his dress uniform with the 1872-pattern officer's blouse with the shoulder straps of a second lieutenant of cavalry. *BP*

Left: DeRudio was later promoted to first lieutenant and in this rank commanded Company A during the Little Bighorn battle. Here he wears the shoulder knots of a first lieutenant and has fitted himself out with an 1872-pattern officer's forage cap with correct leather chinstrap, as well as draping a cape over his right shoulder. He lived until 1910. *LBBNM*

Right: Lieutenant Winfield Scott Edgerly was one of those who saddled up and followed Company D's commander, Thomas Weir, on a pell-mell ride to locate Custer during the battle. Thinking better of this rash act, the men soon turned around and beat a hasty retreat to Major Marcus Reno's entrenched position to survive the battle. Edgerly has removed all insignia and turned back the lapels of his dress coat to reveal his studded shirt. *GS*

Left: Captain Thomas French of M Company has provided himself with a dark blue wool dress cape, dark leather gloves, and what appears to be an elaborate watch fob to accent his 1872-pattern dress uniform. *LBBNM*

Above: Here French appears with his 1872-pattern officer's forage cap, sans chinstrap. French survived the battle. *GS*

Above right: Company H's First Lieutenant Francis Marion Gibson wears a pair of fine gauntlets in this O.S. Goff image. Gauntlets were not issued to enlisted men until 1883, but most officers provided themselves with a pair. Gibson commanded Company G in the battle, and lived to 1919. *GS*

Right: First Lieutenant Edward Godfrey commanded Company K in 1876 and lived to a ripe old age, dying in 1932. The pronounced weave of Godfrey's bullion chest cord for his 1872-pattern dress uniform is typical of the 1870s. *GS*

Left: Company K's Second Lieutenant Luther Rector Hare could almost be mistaken for a civilian were it not for the officer's side stripe on his trousers. Officers were permitted to wear dark blue coats of quasi-military or civilian cut when not performing duties. Hare survived the battle and died in 1929. *GS*

Above: Second Lieutenant Charles Larned was one of the 'Custer Avengers' brought in to replace those officers killed at the Little Bighorn. His chest cords are draped upon his uniform in a haphazard fashion, typical for officers of the time. *GS*

Opposite page: Second Lieutenant Benjamin Hubert Hodgson of Company B wears the complete 1872 dress uniform as prescribed. Great attention was paid to the tailoring of these uniforms as evident by the fact that Hodgson's outfit is form fitting. He died at the Little Bighorn. *LBBNM*

Left: Captain Charles Stilliman Isley of Company E was an aide-de-camp to Brigadier General John Pope during the Little Bighorn Campaign, and thus wears an aiguillette on the right shoulder similar to W.W. Cooke's. His gauntlets are identical in detail to a pair owned by Custer that are now found in the collection of the Smithsonian Institution. Isley died in 1899. *LBBNM*

Above: First Lieutenant Donald McIntosh of Company G was not photographed frequently. Here he has on a forage cap instead of his dress helmet, a substitution that was permitted in those instances where officers were not serving with troops or carrying on strictly military duties. *LBBNM*

Left: Captain Thomas Mower McDougall of Company B shows the predilection for some officers to adopt larger, non-regulation sleeve lace. Also note that for this photograph he wears the tassels of his chest cord on the incorrect side of the uniform. McDougall survived the battle. *GS*

Left: Captain Myles Moylan of Company A wears the 1875-pattern officer's fatigue blouse buttoned only at the top, an affectation considered *de rigueur*, to reveal a pale vest and watch fob. Officers were permitted vests of blue or cream color by regulations. Moylan survived the battle. *GS*

Below: Second Lieutenant Andrew Humes Nave of Company I, seated in the center of this group portrait taken at Fort McKeen, Dakota Territory, in 1873, wears his 1872-pattern dress helmet and berlin gloves. The remainder of the officers are from the Seventeenth U.S. Infantry, and the diversity of their dress and campaign uniform demonstrates that officers of the 1870s tended toward a range of personally-selected outfits regardless of the regiment or branch. *GS*

Right: First Lieutenant Henry James Nowlan served as the regimental quartermaster at the time of the battle. Note the large cuffs of his stylish gauntlets and the medals he received from his prior service in the British Army during the Crimean War. *LBBNM*

Left: First Lieutenant James Ezekiel Porter of Company I strikes a familiar pose. Sitting on the table to his left is his 1872-pattern officer's dress helmet, an unusual example in that the plume base points fore and aft as opposed to the accepted pattern. This detail and the squat appearance of the helmet identifies it as one made by Baker and McKinney, a New York-based military outfitter. Porter was killed at Little Bighorn. *GS*

Left: Major Marcus Albert Reno's 1872-pattern helmet is next to him in this portrait that also shows the field grade officer's dress belt clearly, this item differing from those for company grade officers in that the three rows of yellow silk stripes were eliminated and the lace was plain bullion. *WP*

Opposite page: Second Lieutenant James Garland Sturgis of Company M was the son of the regimental commander, Colonel Samuel Davis Sturgis. Lieutenant Sturgis was killed on 25 June 1876 – less than a year after he accepted his appointment to the Seventh Cavalry. *GS*

Right: Here Reno has removed his belt and helmet and holds his forage cap, which once again is without a chinstrap. The three stripes of gold lace on his cuffs and the nine buttons in each row of his 1872-pattern dress coat were the prescribed means to set off field grade from company grade officers. Reno was one of five field grade officers serving with the Seventh at the time of the Little Bighorn Campaign, but only Custer and he were present at the battle. Reno survived, but not without accusations from some quarters that he was to blame for the defeat. *GS*

Left: Detail of a company grade officer's 1872-pattern dress saber belt lace from the *Annual Report of the Secretary of War* published in 1876.

Below: Second Lieutenant George Daniel Wallace was with Company G, but after the Little Bighorn he replaced Cooke as regimental adjutant, as indicated by the complicated aiguillettes that distinguished this position. *GS*

Opposite page: Captain Thomas Bell Weir of Company D sets off his 1872-pattern company grade officer's dress uniform with a pair of elegant thigh-high boots. Such footgear was more common during the Civil War, and recalled visions of romantic European cavaliers which so enamored many Victorians. *GS*

Left: In this view Weir has evidently converted an enlisted man's overcoat by the addition of dark astrakhan applied to the collar. *GS*

Below: Elaborate black silk galloons applied to the cuffs of the 1851-pattern officer's cloakcoa or capote were the marks of a general officer. Custer (front left) has also added non-regulatio astrakhan trimming to the cuffs and collar of his overcoat. The other officers, Colonel G.A. Forsyth, Lieutenant General P.H. Sheridan, Majo M.V. Ashe, Lieutenant Colonel N.B. Sweitzer, Major M.V. Sheridan, and Lieutenant Colonel J.W. Forsyth (left to right), likewise exhibit modified uniforms with elements of civilian clothing worn with military insignia, buttons, and other regulation accessories. Note the quatrefoil atop General Sheridan's forage cap. The image dates from around January 1872. *LBBNM*

Opposite page: The astrakhan addition to the collar of Custer's 1851-pattern officer's overcoat is also evident in this late 1871 or early 1872 cabinet card. Here he has combined civilian attire with components of the military uniform once more. *GS*

Left: Since ancient times, armies in foreign lands have adopted the dress of the local populace, an affectation declaring both supremacy and respect. So it was with the U.S. Army on the Plains. No single military figure became as identified with 'frontier buckskin' as the flamboyant Custer. In this 9 February 1868 photo taken at Fort Sill, Indian Territory (Oklahoma), a bearded Custer wears what would becom a trademark campaign garment – a double-breasted buckskin coat. While superficially resembling an Indian shirt, Custer's buckskins were sewn, usually machined, by his tailor – a Seventh Cavalry soldier and are patterned on the military styles of the day Although he posed in numerous similar coats, Custer wore this particular coat on all his campaigns, and almost certainly on 25 June 1876. *LBBNM*

Right: This 1872 portrait, taken during a visit by Grand Duke Alexis of Russia, shows the same coat, this time being combined with Custer's trademark red scarf – a still potent symbol of his stature as a Civil War era icon. The modified M1868 .50-70 caliber Springfield rifle was one of several used by Custer's close friends at Fort Leavenworth, Kansas. *GS*

Right: Surrounded by his scouts (including Bloody Knife at his right and Goose standing behind his camp chair), his striker (or batman) John Burkman, and his prized hunting hounds, this 1874 image shows Custer again sporting a beard and his veteran buckskin coat. Featured prominently are a rolling block Remington rifle and two newly-acquired Colt Single Action Army revolvers. Note the four-button fatigue jacket worn by Goose. *LBBNM*

Right: Taken during the Black Hills Expedition of 1874, Custer's first grizzly bear kill is documented here, with the buckskin-clad Captain William Ludlow taking part in the photo session. Also present are Bloody Knife and Seventh Cavalry Private John Nunan (also known as Noonan, Nonen, and Nuwnen). Nunan wears the short-lived 1872-pattern pleated blouse while Bloody Knife has on the so-called, 'Fair-weather Christian' belt. Such cartridge belts were in common use long before the army conceded their utility and reluctantly began to issue them in late 1876. *LBBNM*

Above left: As evident in this *circa* 1875 picture, New Yorker John Briody, a corporal in Company F, opted to convert the roll collar of the old style four-button sack by adding what may be a velvet covering. He also had a convenient exterior breast pocket tailored into the blouse which he may have worn into the field at Little Bighorn, where he was killed.

Above: Private William O. Tyler of the Seventh U.S. Cavalry sat for the photographer in his 1872 pattern cavalry enlisted dress coat and 1872-pattern forage cap. All facings were to be yellow in contrast to the dark blue material of the coat. *GM*

Left: The Seventh U.S. Cavalry's regimental standard of the 1866–87 era. The cloth is of blue silk with painted Arms of the United States and survived the battle because it was stored with the pack train rather than being carried into combat. *LBBNM*

Right: This corporal of the Seventh Cavalry follows the 1872–81 regulations for dress uniforms. The long front and back visors of his helmet are evident, as are the regulation brass collar numerals which indicate his unit. Trim on the cuffs and shoulder loops is of yellow facing material, as is the 4-inch horizontal patch affixed to both sides of the collar. Yellow piping likewise ran around the top and bottom of the collar and down the front seams and along the skirt, which was slit at the sides for mounted troops. The horsehair plume and one-piece worsted helmet cords were to be yellow to match the chevrons, and ½-inch leg stripes were called for on trousers of corporals. *BB*

Left: The enlisted man's 1872-pattern cavalry dress helmet had yellow one-piece worsted cords and a yellow horsetail plume to match the trim of the coat. The collar was to display a pair of stamped sheet brass regimental numbers, one on each side, in this instance for the Seventh U.S. Cavalry. *MJM*

Opposite page: Sergeant Jeremiah Finley of Company C was among the many Irishmen who rode to the strains of *Garry Owen* at the Little Bighorn. A veteran of the Union army, he was a tailor as well as a soldier, and made the buckskin jacket Custer wore to his death, a fate which the sergeant shared. He appears in the 1872-pattern enlisted man's dress uniform. *GS*

Right: Officer's type brass snaps on his saber slings and the M1872 leather saber knot are two features of Daniel A. Kanipe's accoutrements. Also note the black japanned pinwheel ventilators on the side of his 1872-pattern enlisted man's helmet. *Montana Historical Society*

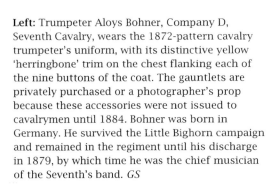

Left: Trumpeter Aloys Bohner, Company D, Seventh Cavalry, wears the 1872-pattern cavalry trumpeter's uniform, with its distinctive yellow 'herringbone' trim on the chest flanking each of the nine buttons of the coat. The gauntlets are privately purchased or a photographer's prop because these accessories were not issued to cavalrymen until 1884. Bohner was born in Germany. He survived the Little Bighorn campaign and remained in the regiment until his discharge in 1879, by which time he was the chief musician of the Seventh's band. *GS*

Above: Not long after the June 1876 battle at the Little Bighorn, men of Company B, Seventh U.S. Cavalry, gathered for this group portrait in their 1872 dress uniforms. *GS*

Left: William O. Tyler's July 1872 portrait shows he has been issued an 1872-pattern enlisted forage cap, which he wears in tandem with a Civil War era four-button enlisted blouse and 1861-pattern sky-blue kersey trousers. This combination was seen in garrison and to some extent in the field into the mid-1870s. *GM*

Below: The unpopularity of the 1872-pattern hat and blouse eventually brought about the discontinuance of these items and their replacement. Sergeant Benjamin Criswell of Company B here shows a specially tailored 1874-pattern enlisted blouse which he combines with a privately purchased black cravat and 'boiled' (starched) white shirt for this photograph taken around 1875 or 1876. He has also elected to have custom-made chevrons fashioned of separately applied stripes, rather than the single piece of yellow facing cloth outlined in black silk chainstitch to form the stripe as adopted as standard in 1872. *LBBNM*

Above: In addition to the new pleated field blouse adopted in 1872, as worn here by Private Howard Weaver, Troop A, Seventh Cavalry, an 1872-pattern folding campaign hat began to be issued for field service. Neither item was particularly popular with the troops. *GM*

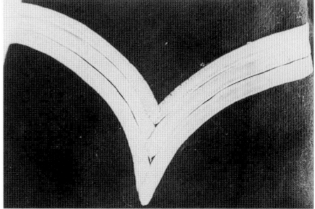

Above: Sergeant William William's dress coat has had custom chevrons applied, similar to those worn by other non-commissioned officers in the Seventh Cavalry during the 1870s. *LBBNM*

Left: Miles O'Hara, seen here as a corporal, had gullwing chevrons of yellow facing material, which while not issue, were typical of the early 1870s period and favored by some non-commissioned officers in the Seventh Cavalry. They were separately applied pieces of yellow cloth sewn on the sleeve of his 1874-pattern enlisted blouse, a garment that was to replace the previous pleated version. The yellow cord piping on the cuff of the jacket faintly shows in this image. Also note the three buttons on the cuff. Although the official pattern had only one button, the addition of up to three buttons was not uncommon. The 1872-pattern forage cap bears the old 1858-pattern cavalry crossed saber insignia. Finally, O'Hara has purchased a vest that is set off by a watch fob. *LBBNM*

Left: Trooper Korn holds Comanche, the 'brave horse', by the reins. The saddle is a leather-covered Jennifer type and sits on an officer's cheverac that typically was edged in yellow leather with a yellow leather numeral applied. Comanche was the mount of Captain Keogh and was wounded at Little Bighorn. Korn has on the 1874-pattern enlisted man's blouse and 1872-pattern forage cap. *GS*

All the privates in this picture have donned their 'walking out' outfits with a variety of individual touches. All wear the 1874-pattern blouse with the 1872-pattern forage cap, although the caps bear smaller non-regulation sabers in three of the four cases that will have been private purchases. The small brass company letters above the sabers are regulation size, however, as of 1872, although not until the middle of the decade did general orders clarify the manner of wearing these unit identifications. Also note that the man on the left, Musician George Penwell, has three buttons on the cuff of his blouse, rather than the one that was to be found on the specimen kept by the Quartermaster General's Department as the standard. In addition, Penwell has added double ½-inch stripes apparently applied to a piece of dark cloth and then sewn to the trousers. The practice of wearing double stripes finally became regulation for trumpeters and musicians in 1883, after many years of traditional use. *LBBNM*

Right: John McGuire's 1874-pattern blouse and 1872-pattern forage cap with stamped sheet brass crossed sabers and regimental as well as company insignia follow the 1872 regulations and the 1875 placement of insignia. His accoutrements are typical of those worn in garrison, including the 2½-inch wide black leather carbine sling that ran from the left shoulder to right hip, to keep the .45 caliber Springfield 'trapdoor' carbine with the trooper at all times. *LBBNM*

Left: William O. Tyler of the Seventh U.S. Cavalry also has on the 1874-pattern five-button blouse that replaced the 1872-pattern pleated blouse. His hat may be the 1876-pattern campaign hat, or possibly a civilian slouch hat that he has fitted out with stamped brass crossed sabers and regimental numeral along with the 1858-pattern yellow worsted hat cords. The addition of such items to the hat, although not unknown, tended to be rather limited in practice. *GM*